AMAZON FIRE TV STICK USER GUIDE

The Ultimate Amazon Fire TV Stick User Manual

Tom Collins

Table of contents

Introduction

Amazon entered the crowded area of streaming set-height boxes. But while the Fire TV sounded like a genuine success on paper, in practice it was more of a mixed bag. The internet retail giant scaled back its ambitions and the cost. The Fire TV Stick is a streaming dongle similar to the Chromecast or Roku Streaming Stick that's focused mainly on serving up video and less on gaming. Plus, the $39 price tag dramatically lowers the bar for entering. But, even at less than half the price, the Fire TV Stick would be a tough pill to swallow if Amazon didn't iron out some of the kinks from its first-generation device. So has a few more months of polish addressed our concerns about Fire OS on the big screen? Without throwing too much away, the result is generally yes.

The Fire TV Stick addresses a number of issues we had with the Fire TV and comes with a much smaller price tag. It's not dramatically better than its competitors, but it's certainly not any worse. For $39, it's a perfectly viable streaming-media option, and the best one if you've already bought into the Amazon's ecosystem. This user guide not only addresses several issues of the amazing amazon fire TV stick but also proffer solutions where necessary.

Do I really need an amazon prime?

Amazon Prime is an Amazon's membership that guarantees you access to all sorts of services and other benefits.

For those not familiar with Amazon Prime, one yearly payment of $99 will get you free access to Amazon Prime Video, Prime Music, Prime Photos, the Kindle Lending Library, free two-day shipping on certain items, and discounted next-day shipping on certain items.

That's a lot of benefit for just $99 per year which is equivalent to $8.25 per month. Of course, the $99 price tag does make some users scared and that's not surprising, as $99 is a lot of money to pay up front for anything.

However, that price gets you a lot of stuff that would normally cost a lot more if you had to pay for all of them individually, and if you shop on Amazon a lot, that free two-day shipping can easily pay for itself in a year's time.

Difference between Fire TV Stick and Fire TV

Amazon officially launched its Fire TV Stick thereby joining the company's lineup of hardware products and sitting pretty as a cheaper alternative to the Fire TV, but what are the differences between the two streaming devices?

The Fire TV from Amazon is a full-fledged streaming box that aims to compete with the Apple TV, Roku, and the Nexus Player, but the Fire TV Stick is also a standalone streaming box that gives users access to all sorts of content, but in a smaller form factor.

Both streaming devices from Amazon are headlined by the company's Prime Instant Video streaming service, and it's baked into the main functionality of the two devices, but users can also access other streaming sources like Netflix, Hulu Plus, and more. You may think that there's not much difference between the Fire TV and the Fire TV Stick, but the functionality between the two devices is something that separates the two from each other, even though they may look the same from the surface.

If you're looking to buy a streaming device for yourself or as a Christmas gift for that special someone, you may want to know what the differences are between the Fire TV and the Fire TV Stick. Here's what you need to know.

Price and Value

Arguably the biggest difference between the two systems is how much they cost. The full-fledged Fire TV retails for

$99, while the Fire TV Stick costs just $39. There's no one-size-fits-all advice for which of the two to buy, but generally speaking, I found that the Fire TV Stick was a perfectly good product without the box's bells and whistles.

If you need an Ethernet connection, high-quality audio, core gaming capabilities and built-in voice search, the Fire TV box is the way to go. Otherwise, save yourself a little money and get its smaller, cheaper cousin.

Size

One of the main obvious differences between the Fire TV and the Fire TV Stick is the size of the two devices. The Fire TV comes in a normal size that's comparable to the Apple TV and Roku. It's a simple box that's a few inches across.

The Fire TV Stick, on the other hand, is a small HDMI dongle that plugs into the back of your television and remains out of sight - a perfect solution for those who already have a crowded home entertainment setup in their living room. Plus, the Fire TV Stick is great for portability, and you can simply throw it in your bag and take it with you to another TV.

Ports

If you pick up an Amazon Fire TV Stick, one end connects to an HDMI port, and one connects to a USB port or an outlet. That's all you need to know. Video and audio both come via HDMI. The device uses Wi-Fi to connect to the Internet and Bluetooth for its remote and optional controller.

The Fire TV box, on the other hand, is a much more versatile device. In addition to HDMI and power ports, it also has an Ethernet port, an optical audio out port and a USB port. If the intended recipient does not use Wi-Fi or has a high-end speaker system, the Fire TV box is the better option.

Voice Search and Remote

One of the Fire TV's most touted features is its voice search, which lets users find movies, TV shows, music and games just by speaking into a remote control or a smartphone. While our reviewers had mixed luck with voice search, it's still an advantage the Fire TV has over competitors such as the Chromecast and the Roku stick.

The Fire TV box comes with a premium remote control that includes voice search capabilities. The remote control for the Fire TV Stick feels much flimsier, and does not support voice search. Although Fire TV Stick users can buy a voice search remote separately for $30, they're much better off just buying the full Fire TV box at that point.

However, users can employ voice search on either platform thanks to a free smartphone app, currently available for Android and coming soon to iOS. If voice search is a big deal and the recipient does not have a modern smartphone, the Fire TV box is the better option. Otherwise, the stick should be fine.

Fire TV Stick Hardware Basics

Fire TV stick

It includes a micro-USB port meant for power only and also an HDMI connector. The HDMI connector goes directly into your TV or into the included HDMI extender.

USB Cable and Power Adapter

The USB cable is used to connect your Fire TV Stick to a power source. One end of the cable is plugged into the micro-USB port on your Fire TV Stick and the other end is included in the power adapter and a power outlet.

You can also plug the USB cable into a USB port on your TV for power, but using the included power adapter and plugging it into a power outlet is recommended for optimal performance. Note that the USB port cannot be used to connect the Fire TV Stick to computers or other devices.

In case you want to turn off Fire TV Stick, unplug the USB cable from the device or from the power source.

HDMI Extender Cable

This is added to your Fire TV Stick and you can use it to ensure that your Fire TV Stick fits securely into your TV. Your Wi-Fi connection may also be improved by the HDMI extender.

In order to use the HDMI extender, plug the Fire TV Stick into the HDMI extender, and then plug the HDMI extender into an available HDMI port on your TV.

Getting Started with Fire TV Stick

In order to use your Fire TV Stick, the following are needed:

1. An Amazon account: This will enable you to Amazon account to access movies, TV shows, games, music, and apps on Fire TV Stick.
2. A Wireless Internet Connection: You will need a wireless connection to buy, download, and stream content on Fire TV Stick because this is not included.
3. A High-definition TV: The Fire TV Stick is compatible with any high-definition TVs that has a HDMI ports.
4. A Fire TV Stick equipment
   - 2 AAA Batteries (for the remote)
   - Power Adapter
   - USB Power Cable
   - HDMI Extender Cable
   - Amazon Fire TV Remote
   - Fire TV Stick Device

The Remote Layout

A wireless remote is added to your Amazon Fire TV device. It has a 5-way directional track pad that allows you to navigate your device quickly and easily.

You must install the 2 AAA batteries (which is given to you) before the remote can function and pair it with your Amazon Fire TV device.

Also, a third party remote can be paired. In order to do these, go to connect a Bluetooth Accessory to Your Amazon Fire TV. Controls and performance may vary.

Voice

This is used to search for movies, TV shows, games, or apps using voice commands. Voice search uses two built-in microphones to search for items using your voice commands.

Directional Navigation

Right is to move to the right on your TV screen. Moving to the right from the Main Menu allows you to access the content libraries or storefronts such as movies, TV, games, apps, photos, and more.

Left is to move to the left on your TV screen. Moving to the left allows you to return to the Main Menu from any content library or storefront.

Up is to move up

Down to move down.

Select

Used to select an item, function, or category.

Home

This returns you to the Home screen from any screen on your Amazon Fire TV device.

Menu

It shows several functions and settings depending on which screen you are accessing.

Back

It returns you to the previous screen or action.

Rewind/Play/pause/Fast Forward

These control buttons enable you rewind, play, pause, and fast-forward video.

To skip 10 seconds backward or forward, press the rewind or forward button once. Press and hold the rewind or forward button to continue navigating backward or forward in the video. Added presses allow you to cycle through the available speed options.

Home screen

The Home screen includes the Main Menu. This allows you to have access to your account and device settings, along with movie, TV show, game, and app content libraries.

Press the Home button on the remote to return to the Home screen and Main Menu options.

Main Menu option/Description

Search

For searching movies, TV shows, games, apps, music, and music videos from Vevo. Use the remote to search for content titles using voice input or an onscreen keyboard.

Home

Review content recommendations and recent activity.

Recent activity - Includes your recently viewed movies, TV shows, games, Cloud Drive photos/videos, or apps. To remove an item from Recent, navigate to item and then select Remove from Recent.

Featured Movies & TV or Apps & Games - Timely and relevant promotions featured by Amazon and other content providers. You cannot remove items from the Featured listings.

Other Movies, TV, Apps & Games - Automated listings that include Amazon's newest (New Releases, Recently Added to Prime), best (Top Movies, Free Games), or recommended content (Recommended Movies, Recommended TV). You can only remove items from the Recommended Movies and TV listings.

Prime Video

If you are an Amazon Prime member, you can quickly and easily browse the Prime Instant Video library and watch movies and TV shows in this category at no extra cost.

Movies

Rent, buy, and watch movies from the Amazon Instant Video store and some other installed video apps. If you are an Amazon Prime member, you can quickly and easily browse the Prime Instant Video library and watch movies and TV shows in this category at no extra cost.

TV

Buy and watch TV show episodes or seasons from the Amazon Instant Video store and some other installed video apps. If you are an Amazon Prime member, you can quickly and easily browse the Prime Instant Video library and watch movies and TV shows in this category at no extra cost.

Watchlist

Access your Amazon Instant Video Watchlist. Your Watchlist is a list of movies or TV shows you want to buy, rent, or watch later. After you buy or rent the movie or TV show, it is available to stream from your Video Library.

Video Library

Your Video Library includes all of the Amazon Instant Video movies and TV shows you've purchased or are currently renting, but does not include the movies and TV shows that you've watched through Prime Instant Video. Content you purchase is stored in the Cloud and available to stream to your device.

Movies and TV shows from third-party apps, such as Netflix and Hulu, are only accessible directly from the apps, not the Video Library.

Settings Basics

Your Amazon Fire TV device is designed to make most configuration settings automatic, but you can use the Settings menu to further manage your apps, Internet connection, controllers, screen savers, and more.

From the Home screen, select Settings.

You can quickly access Settings by pressing and holding the Home button on your remote or on the most recent version of the Fire TV Remote App.

Setting/Description

Display and Sounds

Set a screen saver, configure the display, mirror a compatible device, and manage audio settings.

Second Screen Notifications: Enable discovery of Amazon Instant Video playback and Photos on Amazon Fire TV device from nearby compatible mobile devices.

Parental Controls

Parental Controls restrict purchasing, content types, and access to other features.

Parental Controls will not restrict content in third party applications. Parental controls for third-party applications are determined by the app provider.

<u>*Controllers and Bluetooth Devices*</u>

Add, unpair, or update remotes and Bluetooth game controllers. View paired remote apps and third party remotes.

<u>*My Account*</u>

Register or deregister your Amazon Fire TV device with your Amazon account. You can also select Sync Amazon Content to make sure your latest content purchases are available on your device.

Display Mirroring

You can wirelessly display your compatible phone or tablet screen and audio on your Amazon Fire TV device. You can mirror your display most phones or tablets that are Miracast capable. Some capable devices include:

- Fire phone
- Fire HDX Tablets
- Devices running Android 4.2 (Jelly Bean) or higher. Performance may vary.

Before you begin, make sure your Amazon Fire TV device and Miracast capable device are turned on and within 30 feet of each other. If you're using a device that is not registered to the same Amazon account as the Amazon Fire TV device, connect to the same Wi-Fi network as the Amazon Fire TV device.

To quickly start display mirroring, on your Amazon Fire TV remote press and hold the Home button and select Mirroring. Then connect your compatible device.

Device/Steps

Compatible Fire HDX Tablet

1. Swipe down from the top of the screen to open Quick Settings, and then tap Settings.

2. Tap Display & Sounds, and then tap Display Mirroring.

3. Select your Amazon Fire TV device. It may take up to 20 seconds for your Fire Tablet screen to appear on your TV

screen. To stop mirroring your Fire Tablet, tap Stop Mirroring.

Fire phone

1. Open Quick Actions.
2. Under Display select Share your screen via Miracast.
3. Select your Amazon Fire TV device. It may take up to 20 seconds for your Fire phone screen to appear on your TV screen.
4. Tap Stop Mirroring to stop mirroring the screen of your phone.

Android device running 4.2 or higher

1. On your Amazon Fire TV device, select Settings > Display and Sounds > Enable Display Mirroring.
2. On your Miracast-certified device, connect to your Amazon Fire TV. Contact technical support for your device for more information on connecting.
3. Press any button on the remote to stop Display Mirroring.

Listen to Music

Browse and stream the music from Your Music Library with your Amazon Fire TV device, including songs you purchased from the Digital Music Store, imported to Your Music Library, or Prime Music content added to your Music Library. Use Voice Search to quickly find artists, albums, and songs in your library.

To stream Amazon Music, your Amazon Fire TV device must be authorized to your Amazon account. You can have up to 10 devices authorized to your account, and each device can only be authorized to one Amazon Music account at a time.

If you are an Amazon Prime member, you can listen to Prime Music at no additional cost. The Digital Music Store is currently not available on Amazon Fire TV devices. However, you can stream music that you have already purchased or imported from a computer or other device to Your Music Library.

1. From the Home screen, select Music.
2. Browse for music in the Recently Played list, or browse by Playlists, Artists, Albums, or Genres. Use the alphabet above the music to browse quickly.

You can also use Voice Search to search your music. Press and hold the Voice button on the remote, and then say an artist's name, album title, playlist title, or song title.

3. Select a playlist, artist, album, or song to start playing. Use the playback controls on the remote

or in the Fire TV Remote App to play, pause, forward, or rewind the music.

Listen to Prime Music with an Amazon Fire TV Device from your Amazon Fire TV device, you can listen to Prime Music.

To listen to Prime Music, you must be an active Prime member.

To listen to Prime Music:

1. From the Home screen, select Music.
2. Select Your Prime Playlists or browse to a Prime Album in Your Albums. Hold the Voice button, and then say an artist's name, album title, playlist title, or song title.
3. Select a playlist, artist, album, or song to start playing. Use the playback controls on the remote or Fire TV Remote App to play, pause, forward, or rewind the music.

View Photos & Personal Videos

Any photos and personal videos you upload to Amazon Cloud Drive are automatically available on your Amazon Fire TV device when you register your Amazon account. You can also display photos and personal videos from some Fire Tablets and Fire phone.

1. To view photos and personal videos from your Cloud Drive:
   a. From the Home screen, select Photos.
   b. Navigate the lists:
      - All - Scroll right and left to view thumbnails of all of your photos and videos. Use the filters at the top to jump to a specific year or month. Select a photo or video to view the full-sized version, and then scroll right and left to continue viewing the full-sized versions of your photos and videos.
      - Press the Back button on your remote to return to the thumbnails.
      - Favorites - All of the photos or videos that you have added to your Favorites list. To add an item, select Add to Favorites below an individual photo or video. You can also filter by Favorites in an album.
      - Albums - Select an album to view the photos and videos in it.
      - Videos - Select a video to watch it. Use the playback controls on the remote to pause, play, rewind, and forward.

2. To display photos and personal videos directly from your compatible device:
    a. Note: Compatible Fire devices include:
        - Kindle Fire HD 2nd Generation
        - Kindle Fire HDX
        - Fire HD 6
        - Fire HD 7
        - Amazon Fire phone

    From your device, tap Photos.

    b. Swipe from the left edge of the screen, and select a category or album.
    c. Tap the Second Screen icon at the top to display your photos and/or videos on your TV.

Shop for, buy, download, and uninstall games and apps from your Amazon Fire TV device.

Games and apps

To buy or download games and apps, you need to have a 1-Click payment method set up.

1. Locate the game or app you want to buy. Browse the categories under Games or Apps. Or search for a game or app with an app or remote:
   - Amazon Fire TV Remote: Select Search from the Home screen and use the onscreen keyboard to enter search terms.
   - Amazon Fire TV Voice Remote: Press the Voice button on your remote to search using your voice or press up. Or select Search from the Home screen to use an onscreen keyboard.
   - Fire TV Remote App: Press and hold the Voice icon, drag the icon down, and then say the name of a game or app. You can also tap the Keyboard icon to use an onscreen keyboard.
2. From your search results, select a game or app to view its overview page. On the overview page, you can see the Works with box. Here you can see system and controller compatibility:

- All
- Fire TV Stick (only visible on Fire TV Stick)
- Fire TV Remote (both Amazon Fire TV Remote and Amazon Fire TV Voice Remote)
- Amazon Fire Game Controller
- Tablet Games on Fire TV (requires a game controller or mouse)
- To learn more about compatible game controllers, visit www.amazon.com/mfkcontrollers

3. Select Buy, or if the app is free, select Free. You can choose to purchase your game or app with your 1-Click payment method or any Amazon Coins you have in your account. Once purchased, your game or app automatically begins downloading. When the download is complete, the button will change to Open.

4. Select Open to being using your game or app. The games or apps you purchase are available in Your Games Library or Your Apps Library on the main Games or Apps screens.

You can uninstall games and apps from your Amazon Fire TV device or USB storage. Games and apps you purchased and uninstalled can be reinstalled again from the game or app overview page.

1. From the Home screen, select Settings > Manage All Applications. To see apps that are only store in USB Storage or on your device select USB Storage or Fire TV.

2. Scroll up or down to find the app you want to uninstall, and select it.

3. Select Uninstall, and then follow the onscreen
    instructions.

Troubleshooting advice

Try these troubleshooting steps for resolving issues like a frozen screen, app errors, or problems with content such as movies, TV shows, games, and apps.

Issue/Try this

There is video but no sound

- Make sure the TV audio is not muted.
- If the Amazon Fire TV device is connected to an AV receiver, make sure it is on.
- From the Home screen, go to Settings > Display and Sounds > Dolby Digital Output and make sure Dolby Digital Plus is set to OFF.

The Amazon Fire TV device is on, but nothing is on the screen

- Make sure the TV is on and set to the correct channel and/or HDMI input.
- If the Amazon Fire TV device is connected through an A/V receiver, connect it directly to the TV.
- Disconnect other devices from your TV's HDMI ports.
- Try setting the TV to a different resolution (1080P or 720P).
- On the remote, press Up and Rewind together for 5 seconds. The Amazon Fire TV device will cycle through the possible output resolutions, starting with 1080p and working its way down to 480p,

pausing at each resolution for 10 seconds. On the Amazon Fire TV, the indicator light will blink yellow. If you see the correct resolution, select Use Current Resolution.

Problems purchasing or accessing content

- Confirm that your Amazon Fire TV device is connected to the Internet. An Internet connection is re□uired to buy, stream, and sync your content.
- Verify that you are connected to the Internet by visiting Home, select Settings > System > Wi-Fi.
- Verify that your 1-Click payment method is set up correctly. To learn more, go to Change your 1-Click Settings.

Movies, photos, or purchased content not showing

Verify that your Amazon Fire TV device is registered to the correct Amazon account. Basic Troubleshooting for Amazon Fire TV Devices

To verify your registration, go to the Home screen, select Settings > My Account. If you see the wrong account listed, select Deregister. Then select Register to register the correct account.

Specific app issues

1. From the Home screen, select Settings > Applications > Manage All Installed Applications.
2. Select the application you want to modify. You can now:
   - Change settings

- Move the app between internal and USB storage (Amazon Fire TV only)
- Clear data
- Clear cache
- Force stop
- Uninstall the application

Can't Access USB Storage

1. Make sure you are using a supported USB device. Go to About USB Storage for Amazon Fire TV.
2. Eject the USB storage. Go Settings > System > USB Storage > Eject. Wait for the confirmation before safely removing the device.
3. Remove the USB device and plug it back in.

Alexa on Fire TV stick

In addition to voice search, you can use your Fire TV voice remote or remote app to interact with Alexa.

Just press and hold the Voice button, and ask for information, music, audiobooks, news, weather, traffic, sports, and more. Alexa then answers back directly through your Fire TV. Many features open in a separate display on your TV screen, so you can both see and hear Alexa in action.

At this time, Alexa is only available on Amazon Fire TV devices running Fire OS software version 5 or higher and Fire TV Stick devices running Fire OS 5.0.3 or higher. To check the software version currently installed on your device, open Settings > System > About. We're working to bring Alexa to other Amazon Fire TV devices with an upcoming software release.

Manage Alexa Features

You can set and manage settings for some Alexa features using our free Amazon Alexa App) for Fire OS, Android, iOS, and supported desktop web browsers.

For more information, including installation instructions, go to download the Amazon Alexa App.

When an Alexa display is open on your TV screen, press the Back Button or Home button on your Fire TV remote to return to the previous screen.

Made in the USA
Monee, IL
08 July 2026